KT-482-241

CARDIFF
CAERDYDD

Cardiff Libraries
www.cardiff.gov.uk/libraries

Llyfrgelloedd Caerdy
www.caerdydd.gov.uk/llyfrgelloec

ACC. No: 05004316

Fact Finders®

WHAT YOU NEED TO KNOW ABOUT
CONCUSSIONS

BY KRISTINE CARLSON ASSELIN

raintree
a Capstone company — publishers for children

Raintree is an imprint of Capstone Global Library Limited, a company incorporated in England and Wales having its registered office at 7 Pilgrim Street, London, EC4V 6LB – Registered company number: 6695582

www.raintree.co.uk
myorders@raintree.co.uk

Text © Capstone Global Library Limited 2016
The moral rights of the proprietor have been asserted.

All rights reserved. No part of this publication may be reproduced in any form or by any means (including photocopying or storing it in any medium by electronic means and whether or not transiently or incidentally to some other use of this publication) without the written permission of the copyright owner, except in accordance with the provisions of the Copyright, Designs and Patents Act 1988 or under the terms of a licence issued by the Copyright Licensing Agency, Saffron House, 6–10 Kirby Street, London EC1N 8TS (www.cla.co.uk). Applications for the copyright owner's written permission should be addressed to the publisher.

Developed and produced by Focus Strategic Communications, Inc.
Edited by Brenda Haugen and Helen Cox Cannons
Designed by Steve Mead
Picture research by Svetlana Zhurkin
Production by Victoria Fitzgerald
Originated by Capstone Global Library Limited
Printed and bound in China

ISBN 978 1 474 70397 0 (hardback)
19 18 17 16 15
10 9 8 7 6 5 4 3 2 1

British Library Cataloguing in Publication Data
A full catalogue record for this book is available from the British Library.

Acknowledgements
We would like to thank the following for permission to reproduce photographs:
Alamy: Nucleus Medical Art Inc, 7, Sherry Moore, 17; Corbis: Colorsport, 5; Dreamstime: Jaco Janse Van Rensburg, 14 (left); iStockphoto: PeopleImages, cover (bottom), 1 (bottom), ScantyNebula, 10 (left), tacojim, 12; Landov: The Plain Dealer/Lisa Dejong, 20; Newscom: Icon Sportswire/YCJ/Andy Mead, 26, Mirrorpix, 25, 29 (top), Rex/Huw Evans, 13; Science Source: Spencer Sutton, 16; Shutterstock: Aspen Photo, 18, Bo Valentino, 10 (middle), Eric Fahrner, 6, everything possible (background), back cover and throughout, Jakkrit Orrasri, 9, Laszlo Szirtesi, 11, Levent Konuk, 8, Lisa F. Young, 21, Mai Techaphan, 4, Monkey Business Images, 22, Paolo Bona, 15, 27, Photographee.eu, 24, Puwadol Jaturawutthichai, cover (top) and throughout, Sergei Butorin, 28, Sinisha Karich, 10 (right), stockpackshot, 29 (bottom), Susan Leggett, 14 (right), Volt Collection, 23.

The publishers would like to thank Lee Goldstein, MD, Ph.D., Associate Professor of Psychiatry and Neurology, Boston University School of Medicine, Boston, Massachusetts for his invaluable help in the making of this book.

Every effort has been made to contact copyright holders of material reproduced in this book. Any omissions will be rectified in subsequent printings if notice is given to the publisher.

All the internet addresses (URLs) given in this book were valid at the time of going to press. However, due to the dynamic nature of the internet, some addresses may have changed, or sites may have changed or ceased to exist since publication. While the author and publisher regret any inconvenience this may cause readers, no responsibility for any such changes can be accepted by either the author or the publisher.

CONTENTS

CHAPTER 1

WHAT IS A CONCUSSION?

It is down to the wire, perhaps the most important moment of the game. The fly-half kicks the ball down the field. The opposing full-back jumps to catch the high ball. Just as he is about to grab it, an opposing player slams into him. Both players fall to the ground.

▼ One rugby player tackles another as the game heats up.

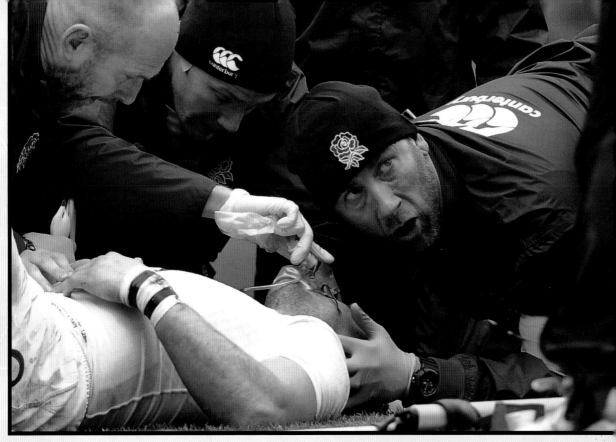

▲ Is this rugby player fit to continue?

Not moving, the player lies flat on the ground. A few minutes later, he sits up. He shakes his head and insists he is fine. He tries to persuade the medical staff to let him finish the game. But when the player stands up, he becomes dizzy. The medical staff decide to **substitute** him.

Even though the player said he was fine, the medical staff could see **symptoms** of concussion. That was why they took him out of the game. This scene is played out across the country in many sports, for both boys and girls.

substitute take one player out of the match and replace with another
symptom something that suggests a person is ill or has a health problem

BRAIN INJURY

A concussion is the result of a sudden injury to the brain. It is sometimes called a **traumatic brain injury** (TBI). A concussion can happen in many ways. It can be caused by any hard fall. It could be a bang to the head. It could even be a violent shake. Any of these can make the brain stop working the way it should.

▼ A hit to the head or a fall on the ice in ice hockey can lead to a concussion.

A concussion can be hard to **diagnose**. If a player does not tell someone how he or she is feeling, the symptoms might not be recognized as a concussion. A second bang to the head, before enough **recovery** time, can cause a more serious injury.

▼ how a concussion happens

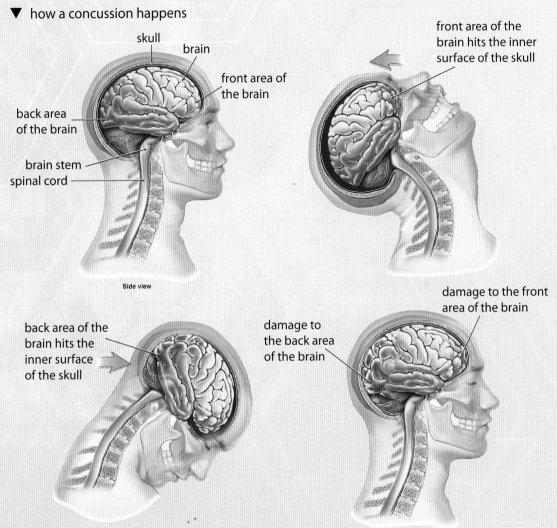

skull

brain

front area of the brain

back area of the brain

brain stem

spinal cord

Side view

front area of the brain hits the inner surface of the skull

back area of the brain hits the inner surface of the skull

damage to the back area of the brain

damage to the front area of the brain

traumatic brain injury violent injury to the brain

diagnose identify a problem, such as a concussion

recovery getting better; returning to health

CHAPTER 2

INVISIBLE INJURIES

A concussion is an invisible injury. Your doctor can easily see and treat a broken bone. But you cannot see a concussion with the naked eye. Even modern technology such as **X-rays** or **MRIs** may not show a concussion.

▼ A technician prepares a patient for an MRI.

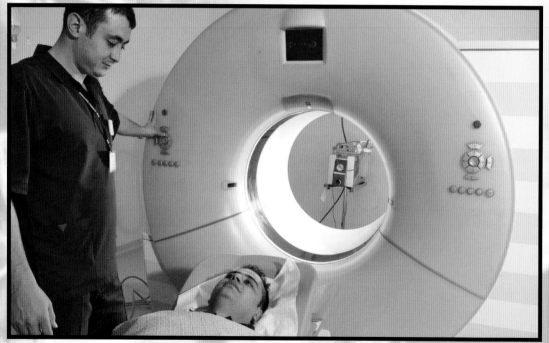

HEALTH FACT

Magnetic resonance imaging (MRI) is a way for doctors to see what is going on inside your body. It uses a giant magnet and radio waves to create a picture. MRIs may "see" problems that might not show up on other tests.

A concussion can be hard to diagnose. Only a doctor or nurse can tell for certain if the brain has been hurt. But coaches and players can watch for signs of concussion. They may notice changes in how a person is feeling, moving, behaving or thinking. The changes may be **physical** or **mental**.

▼ A player is being checked for symptoms of brain injury.

X-ray type of radiation; it takes pictures of the inside of a person's body
MRI medical technique that uses magnets to help take a picture of the inside of a person; MRI stands for magnetic resonance imaging
physical related to the body; something that can be seen or observed
mental related to the mind or brain

Concussion signs

After a bang to the head, most people with a concussion may say they see stars, have a headache or feel dizzy. Sometimes the person loses his or her memory for a few minutes or longer. Over 90 per cent of people with concussions were never actually knocked out. Signs of concussion may include:

- headache
- memory loss
- loss of concentration
- dizziness
- loss of balance
- dilated pupils

- nausea
- vomiting
- blurred vision
- swollen bump
- bruising
- mood swings

- depression
- anxiety
- slurred speech
- difficulty speaking
- sleepiness
- difficulty sleeping

▲ dilated pupil

▲ headache

▲ sleepiness

CAUSES OF CONCUSSION

Any bang or jolt to your head could cause a concussion. You do not have to be playing a contact sport. Even heading a football could cause a concussion. But not every blow does.

▼ Heading a football can sometimes cause a concussion.

Possible ways to get a concussion

Concussions mainly occur during team sports, but there are other ways they can happen too.

- falling off your bike
- getting hit with a football
- being knocked down or tackled
- getting hit with a stick in hockey or lacrosse
- falling off a surfboard, snowboard or skateboard

- getting kicked in the head
- running into a tree on skis
- falling off a horse
- skating into the boards (ice hockey)
- car accident
- playground accident

▼ Falling off a skateboard can result in a concussion.

CONCUSSION STATISTICS

According to Headway, a brain injury association, there were more than 200,000 people taken to hospital with head injuries in the UK in 2011–12. It is believed that most concussions happen during matches, not practices. Perhaps that is because players tend to go all out in a win-or-lose situation.

Awareness is important. In rugby union, the number of concussions reported in 2013–14 increased by 59 per cent compared to the previous season. This is partly because players are now more willing to admit to having concussion. In the past, some players had not wanted to be seen as weak, so would get up and continue playing.

▼ Welsh rugby player Jamie Roberts helps to publicise new Welsh Rugby Union concussion guidelines 2014.

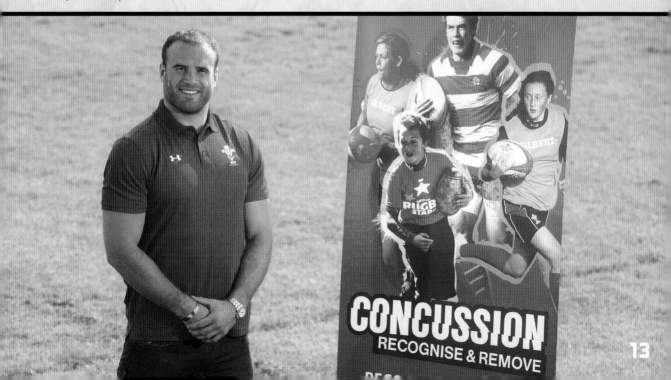

CONCUSSION
RECOGNISE & REMOVE

Concussion rates per sport in the United States

Sport	Concussions per 100,000 athletes
American football	470
Men's football (soccer)	220
Women's football (soccer)	360
Volleyball	50
Men's baseball	70
Women's baseball	210
Wrestling	180
Softball	70

▼ cricket

▼ wrestling

▲ volleyball

ISABELLE'S THREE CONCUSSIONS

Twelve-year-old Isabelle was playing in an exciting basketball match at school. During the last few minutes she and another girl smashed into each other. Isabelle got a concussion. Then she fell to the floor and hit her head. That was concussion number two.

Isabelle's symptoms included headaches, dizziness and difficulty with her balance. Three weeks later she felt better. Her doctor said she could resume her normal activities.

Seven months later Isabelle had her third concussion. She got hit in the head by a hockey stick. She had the same symptoms she had before. But this time her emotions were affected too. She was moody, difficult and often angry with her family. However, as Isabelle got better, all these symptoms disappeared.

CHAPTER 3

DIAGNOSIS

Reports of head injuries to children have increased in recent years. This is partly because people are more aware of TBIs.

In the past, players and coaches did not think concussions were all that serious. No one had much training about them. So children were encouraged to "shake it off" and continue to play. We now know that even a single concussion can damage the brain. If you get a second concussion before the first one has healed, you could cause permanent damage.

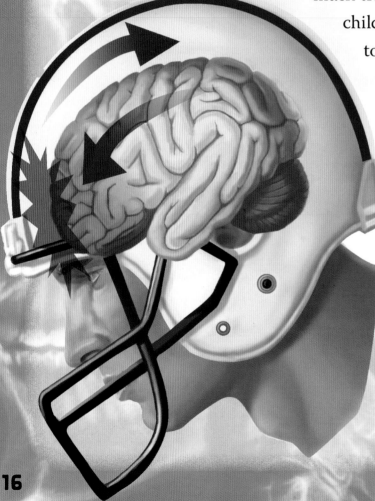

◀ This diagram shows the impact on the brain from a blow to the head.

▲ A coach checks a player for symptoms of concussion.

Today there are better guidelines on handling concussions. However, there is still a lot of debate about what a concussion actually is. Players who have even one concussion symptom are often not allowed to go back into the game.

If a coach or other adult thinks you have a concussion, make sure you follow his or her instructions. If you have a headache or feel dizzy, tell your coach. It is better to be safe than sorry. Having a better understanding of the risks keeps children safer.

DIAGNOSIS CHALLENGE

Players, coaches and parents should know the symptoms of concussion. That way, they can make the right decision on the sidelines. The wrong decision could mean extra weeks or months of recovery for the player. A player's safety is always more important than winning a game. But how does anyone know if a player should continue playing?

▼ The coach must decide if a player should be substituted.

Suppose the player is you. One of the first things your coach may do is ask you to walk in a straight line or count to 10. Or the coach might ask you questions to see if your brain is working properly. If you seem confused or have any other concussion symptoms, you may be **substituted**. The coach will ask you to see a doctor.

Concussion checklist

Unconscious
- Is the player's mouth or throat blocked?
- Is the player breathing normally?
- Is the player's heart beating regularly?

Conscious
- Can the player walk in a straight line?
- Can the player count to 10?
- Can the player answer simple questions?

Actions
- A medical professional assesses the player.
- The player cannot return to the game until a licensed medical professional clears him or her.
- If a concussion is diagnosed, the player is removed from the game immediately.
- The player is to be monitored for 3 or 4 hours after injury (sometimes longer).
- If no concussion is diagnosed, the medical professional may clear the player to return to the game.

HEALTH FACT

To test your memory, a coach or doctor might ask the following questions:
- Where are we?
- What's the colour of the sky?
- What's the score in the game so far?
- Do you remember what happened?

BASELINE TESTING

Doctors now ask athletes to take **baseline tests** before the playing season begins. This is a set of questions and balance tasks. The test records a player's normal reactions to questions and pictures. It also scores some physical reactions.

▼ A research engineer, left, uses a special app to do baseline testing for concussions.

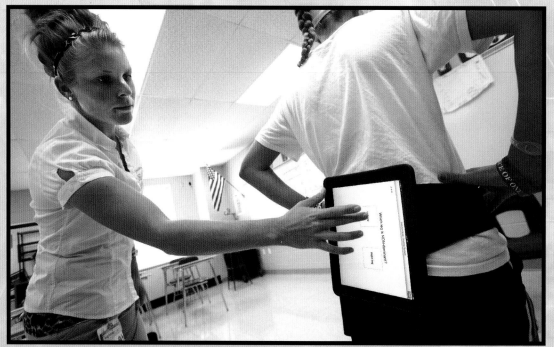

HEALTH FACT

A baseline is a starting point. So a baseline test records an athlete's physical and mental abilities at the starting point of a season.

baseline test basic standard or level test

If a doctor thinks a player has a concussion, the player takes the same baseline test again. The doctor can compare the results to the earlier ones. Having these tests on record can help the doctor diagnose a concussion. It can also help the doctor judge how bad the concussion is.

▼ A doctor compares test results.

TREATMENT

The main treatment for a concussion is resting the brain. This means no activities such as sport, watching TV or playing computer games. You should also avoid bright lights and crowded places. All these put strain on the brain, which can slow your recovery. Only a doctor can tell you how much activity to avoid and for how long.

Most concussion patients recover in a week or two. But a severe concussion can mean months, or even years, of recovery. Patients can usually get back to their normal activities as soon as the symptoms are gone.

▼ Resting is the best treatment for a concussion.

Six steps to recovery

- complete rest – no physical or mental activity until there are no concussion symptoms for at least 24 hours
- light exercise – slow walking, exercise biking or light jogging
- moderate exercise – moderate jogging, exercise biking or weightlifting
- more intense exercise but no contact sports – running, intense exercise biking, weightlifting
- practice – full-contact practice
- play – return to competitive sports

▶ Using a treadmill can help recovery from a concussion.

LONG-TERM EFFECTS

Most people who have had a concussion make a full recovery. But without proper care and rest, the brain takes longer to get back to normal.

Long-term effects of concussion can include trouble sleeping. You may have a hard time focusing in school. You may also experience unusual mood swings.

▼ Anxiety attacks are one possible effect of a concussion.

BRAIN TRAUMA AND FOOTBALL

Jeff Astle, West Bromwich Albion and England footballer, died in 2002 at the age of 59. He was known as a player who frequently headed the ball. In the days when he was playing, balls were made of leather and could become very heavy when wet. In his later years, Astle experienced severe memory problems. After Astle's death, it was found that he had had Chronic Traumatic Encephalopathy (CTE). This is a condition that occurs as a result of many concussions over a long period of time. It is a disease more commonly experienced by boxers.

▼ Jeff Astle was the first British footballer to die as a result of playing football.

CHAPTER 4
PREVENTION

Doctors now know that concussions are serious. Yet not all these injuries are reported. More than half of all school athletes may have suffered at least one concussion.

This is why experts want to see a change in children's sport. Many believe that younger children should play only touch rugby, for example.

Some experts also want players to wear helmets for all contact sports. However, others think that a helmet does little to protect the brain from a concussion. Protecting the brain should be a priority for any sport that has a high risk of concussion.

◀ New technology, such as the ear sensor worn by this footballer, is being developed. The sensor sends information about any impact on the player's brain as and when it happens.

CANTER RUGBY

In New Zealand, young children play a version of touch rugby called canter rugby. It is non-contact rugby, which means that it involves no tackling. Tackling is part of the game responsible for so many injuries. In canter rugby, running with the ball is seen as more important than kicking. It is part of the programme for children as young as three at High School Old Boys rugby club in Christchurch. More than 30 top New Zealand players have played for this club, including Andrew Mehrtens and Dan Carter.

▼ Dan Carter (holding the ball)

PROTECTIVE EQUIPMENT

There is a risk of concussion in any sport. You cannot prevent every injury. But it is important to wear the proper safety gear. It is also important to listen to your coach's rules for safety. In rugby union, for example, a system called Headcase has been introduced to encourage people to learn more about concussion.

Doctors and researchers are still studying the effects of concussion on the brain. With so many people playing, concussions cannot be avoided altogether. But with the right information and the proper equipment, sport can be made safer for everyone.

▼ What safety equipment can you spot on these ice hockey players?

The helmet

Batsmen face an extremely hard cricket ball coming at them, often at speeds of over 130 kilometres (80 miles) an hour. Yet the sport was slow to accept head protection. It was only in the late 1970s that some players began to wear helmets regularly (see photo, above). Early helmets worn were similar to motorbike helmets. Protection for the face was just a piece of easily damaged plastic.

Nowadays, helmets are made from a strong, light plastic lined with energy-absorbing foam and have metal faceguards. In the UK, players under the age of 18 must wear helmets when batting.

▼ old helmet

▼ modern helmet

HEALTH FACT

When young cricketers in an area of Australia were made to wear helmets when playing cricket, the rate of head and face injuries fell from 35 per cent to 4 per cent.

GLOSSARY

baseline test basic standard or level test

diagnose identify a problem, such as a concussion

mental related to the mind or brain

MRI medical technique that uses magnets to help take a picture of the inside of a person; MRI stands for magnetic resonance imaging

physical related to the body; something that can be seen or observed

recovery return to good health

substitute take one player out of the match and replace with another

symptom something that suggests a person is sick or has a health problem

traumatic brain injury violent injury to the brain

X-ray type of radiation; it takes pictures of the inside of a person's body

FIND OUT MORE

BOOKS

Promoting Health and Preventing Disease (The Environment Challenge), Rebecca Vickers (Raintree, 2011)

The Usborne Complete Book of the Human Body, Anna Claybourne (Usborne, 2013)

Traumatic Brain Injury: From Concussion to Coma, Connie Goldsmith (Twenty-First Century Books, 2014)

WEBSITES

www.englandrugby.com/my-rugby/players/player-health/concussion-headcase/players-and-parents

If you play rugby and want to learn more about how to spot the symptoms of concussion, have a look at the Headcase website. You can take an online concussion awareness course to help you play safe.

www.healthforkids.co.uk

Learn about all kinds of illnesses and how to stay healthy.

INDEX